CONVERSATIONS

Interviews taken by Jerry Pinto and Jesal Thacker

Editor **Jerry Pinto**
Book Design **Yashmi Kantak**
Printed by **JAK Printers, Mumbai**

Publisher **Bodhana**

First Edition 2013

ISBN 978-81-907217-0-7
Rs. 250/-

CONVERSATIONS

mehlli gobhai   ganesh haloi   prabhakar kolte

CONTENTS

Preface

It has been from my early college days at Sir J.J School of Arts, that the abstract expressions always interested me more than any other form of expression. In class I would often plunge deeply into observing these art works mainly through books and catalogue's as that was most accessible. Amongst them were art works by Vasudeo Gaitonde, Nasreen Mohamedi, Ram Kumar, Jeram Patel, Mehlli Gobhai, Rajendra Dhavan, Ambadas Khobragade, Ganesh Haloi, Prabhakar Kolte. All of them had a common element, which was that their art was un-identifiable - it was formless in its expression. Reading and studying about them I was routed to Paul Klee, Wassily Kandisky, Mark Rothko, Piet Mondrian and the abstract world – as that's the term to define this art form. I was intrigued and went deeper of which these are just some observations/notations.

Nature has been the constant and only muse for all artistic creation. The artist is initially attracted to the obvious physical beauty of nature, its lustrous forms, colours, textures and over all aesthetic sensibility. By probing deeper the artist begins to see what the normal eye cannot and in the process expands his/her vision. All of them are bearers of this vision that is not visible to the eye but is known to us by some intuitive insight. It is a concrete vision, perception and construction of nature - a reality beyond the physical existence.

This book '*Conversations*' is an effort to come closer to these insights, which with time will form the basis for a strong critical and phenomenal study of art. My time spent with each artist is equally memorable and I am fortunate to share some of these with all of you.

An unconditional gratitude to all artists, critics and curators who have shaped this journey.

Thank you

Jesal Thacker

Conversation with

Mehlli Gobhai

Mumbai 2013

"Everything that makes me Mehlli Gobhai should certainly be in the painting."

A conversation such as this one is a performance.
I am performing the role of interlocutor,
when actually I am asking Mehlli Gobhai, one of India's finest abstract painters and an old friend, to re-enact conversations we have often had before.

At another level, the apparent informality of this conversation is another formality and may be read as the result of much careful effort; Gobhai is a painter who is careful about his words, exacting about his idiom. He will not have me plant words in his mouth, no matter how well I think they reflect his thought process. This is unusual; most other interviewees are happy to have erudition planted on them. Gobhai edits each version seriously, considering the shape of each of his sentences, testing words against his own patterns of speech. These are strengths for now I can claim that Gobhai reads as Gobhai says; or at least, as he believes he says.

This is in direct opposition to the ordinary construct of the interview. Here a stranger (the journalist) walks into the space chosen by another stranger (the subject) and is allowed to ask questions that are both pertinent and impertinent. The resultant conversation is placed before the public as a version of the life of the subject when it is about the life of the interviewer as well.

What questions the interviewer asks may tell us more about her/him than the carefully deodorised - sanitised -manicured - detoxified version presented by the subject. When you're dealing with an old friend however, things can be different. We must stop and retrace our steps; a long friendship will not be denied and often one of us speaks in a kind of verbal shorthand to the other; this too must be rectified because we are now speaking to each other but for an audience. We must somehow give them the feeling that they are eaves dropping while keeping them informed.

Another problem presents itself: if a conversation with Gobhai were ever to walk the straight and narrow, the linear and the direct, none of his friends would be fooled. He is the master of the tangential remark and I must confess that I am no slouch in that department. But the tangent is often a good place from which to see the entire circle and Gobhai's 'tangential remarks' are often rich with associations made with his many lives, with his wide circle of friends and his deep engagements with the arts.

Before I began I made out my list of ideas. My 'things to ask', so to speak. One of them was the old chestnut of Indianness and abstract art. I debated whether to put it in or not. I believe in it as much as I believe in the notion of a single unitary definable notion of Indianness—or art for that matter. However, I have also often found that when I defend what I see as axiomatic, I am forced to think clearly, to think hard. The results often surprise me. But on the way to his studio in South Mumbai, I happened on 'Abstract Painting in India: a personal journey' a catalogue essay he wrote for 'Nothing is Absolute: A journey through abstraction', a show curated by the artist and Ranjit Hoskote for the Jehangir Nicholson Foundation.

He opens his piece with the words:
Kandinsky and Mondrian, acknowledged progenitors of abstract painting in the West , were known to be influenced by their exposure to Theosophy, a spiritual and occult movement by Madame Blavatsky and her followers. Theosophy's study of 'Thought Forms' were some of the first images that gave abstract visual form to various human emotions and states of mind.
Already, India had its own pathways leading to visual abstraction. The urge to abstract in India is a blend of elements that are integral to our culture and way of life.

Later, in the essay, he adds:

The sacred geometry of yantras, formal abstract diagrams of great complexity and significance, are familiar 'anchors' in meditation for the spiritually inclined of the country.
Though never labeled as an art form, they are part of an important root source of visual abstraction in India. They are just one more instance of the openness to an abstract visual language and sensibility that is shared by thousands of people. That answer happened even before the question was asked. And so we began somewhere else on a grey evening in his studio, a boxer lying at our feet in the complete

relaxation that only a well-loved dog can reach, and a Gobhai work-in-progress pulsating with a restless, relentless, demanding energy on the wall behind.

Jerry Pinto: Mehlli, can we begin at a place we have visited several times before, in the course of ordinary conversation. This business of inspiration.

Mehlli Gobhai: It was André Masson who said, "The artist is not inspired. He must inspire the viewer." Knox Martin, my teacher at the Art Students' League, New York, did not think much of the artist being inspired. One of his favourite lines was, "The bartender is never drunk."

JP: One of my roles here is to play devil's advocate, the old Vatican role in which one of the faithful turn interrogator in order to ensure that the faith holds.

If then your work seeks to inspire, you should know what it is you seek, even if it is from the doppelganger as viewer or to put it another way: in a perfect world, as artists, we would create and our creations would be received in precisely the same way as we conceived of them, down to the nuance, down to the last detail.

The efforts we make at naturalness would be transparent but would be applauded. The polemic would be received in the right spirit. Each challenge would be answered. Unfortunately, in the world in which we exist, that doesn't happen. Or perhaps, if you think a little about it, maybe it isn't so unfortunate because each engaged viewer/ reader then reinvents the work.

If you seek not to be inspired, but to inspire, what do you want to inspire? I am asking: what does your painting want?

MG : The challenge is to have the viewer participate in what I felt when I was making the work.

JP : And yet meaning is hidden in your work, obscured by what I sometimes think of as your almost microscopic gaze. You move so close in to the body that you hide what you are showing.

MG : What is hidden fascinates me. Consider the hidden design in nature, the geometry behind a shell or a leaf formation. Why am I excited by dried coconuts and seedpods? Or dolphin skulls?

To me, the best response is when someone says a painting of mine looks as if it had created itself, independent of human intervention. When she visited my studio, Madeleine Burnside, curator of 'Marking Black', a show at the Bronx Museum, New York, said that my work evoked "the moment before ignition."

(*Smiles*) I sometimes feel that the time I take over a work, I do get some help from the rust, the dust, the corrosion.

JP : You do know that for someone who talks so much about organic life processes and such, you have a violent idiolect when you talk about your work.

You often say that you want to brutalise the surface, that you have to take control of it...you're sometimes the conquistador of the canvas.

MG : I don't think I've ever thought of these as words of violence but you're right; the process is violent. I'm very suspicious of people who say they enjoy painting, working with colour, with the sensuousness of the materials.

When people ask me whether I enjoy myself painting, I say: I'm not sure 'enjoy' is the right word. I say I'm rather miserable when I'm painting, but I'm more miserable when I'm not painting. Any fulfillment comes only when the work is finished and you almost wonder whether you did it. And for me, by brutalizing a surface I mean that I try to make it not too easily pleasing.

JP: In my own creative process, I feel that there's always a worm i' the rose. The fulfillment is always vitiated by the thought: now what?

MG: It's a compulsion. Painting is a compulsion. My teacher at the Art Students League, Knox Martin would say that every line you put down, every choice of colour must be made as if it were the one you would make in order to take your next breath. When I put it into words, it sounds rather Romantic. But it is a good definition of the kind of compulsion I am talking about.

JP: You talk often about control. You seek order in the piles of books you stack on chairs, in the arrangement of artefacts along a sideboard. And yet, if there's anyone who recognizes the truth of the third law of thermodynamics which states that the universe is heading towards chaos, it is you.

MG: Giving order to that chaos for the self to survive? A Bengali folk painter showed me a series of drawings or *chakhudun*, that his tribe, the *Jadupattya*, creates specially after they hear that someone has just died in the village they are going to visit.

They would gather the necessary details and do a drawing showing the dead person being tormented by the souls of all the animals he had killed or eaten during his life.

The drawing would be brought to the family where it served some ritual function but only when the painter had been paid, would he put in the eyes.

I understood almost immediately what this meant. No wonder anthropologists often recorded the resistance primitive man showed to photography. The modern world laughed at the idea: how could a photograph steal your soul? And yet, I recall reading about an experiment in the sociology of the image, conducted in America: each student had to bring along a photograph of her or his mother and after discussing how primitive tribes feel about images, they were asked to cut out their mothers' eyes in the photographs. It was only a printed image that they were being asked to deface; yet there was an instinctive resistance to doing it.

This idea of a work of art waking up, of it coming alive, of the *Devi's* eyes being put in as the last touch, when she is transformed from clay to the embodiment of the divine, these have been very important ideas.

For me, a work is done when the painting says, "Now don't touch me."

In a television interview, I remember the painter Philip Guston talking about his process. He said that when he began work, everyone was in the room with him, his friends, his predecessors, his critics. And then as he began to work, they began to leave the room, one by one, until he was alone with his work. But the last step was when he had to leave the room too.

I think this is a difficult step when the painter must withdraw from the painting. I don't want personality smeared all over a work.

I think of Balthus saying, "If you have personality, the best thing to do is to get rid of it". Or of Giacometti spending half an hour walking around at a Tang tomb figure of a woman and saying that "more and more he preferred to anything else the impersonal and objective quality in early art; he had less and less liking for the kind of art where the artist put his own feelings and attitudes into what he was doing." [here Gobhai refers to a notebook and reads from Robin Campbell's personal reminiscences, a quotation that he has copied out in his own handwriting].

JP : And yet it is personality that drives the art world. In its worst form, it's the cult of celebrityhood, the page-three painter, let us call her or him. But let me also put it to you that painters charge for their personality. If I walk into a gallery and see a painting that I like, that I connect to, that resonates with me, I ask, "Whose work is that?" I am rather pleased with myself if it is by someone who already has some reputation in the art world. Or I might walk into a show and see a cruciform work with suggestions of certain occult parts of the body, something that brings to mind sex and death, and I might say, "That's a Mehlli Gobhai."

MG : Everything that makes me Mehlli Gobhai should certainly be in the painting.

After that I would like to have the work speak for itself. As to the operations of the market, in which personality does play a role, I would like to believe that I work at my paintings because I must.

But what would happen if no one in the world responded to my work? That a small percentage of the world, that intelligent viewers, buyers, critics, gallery-owners respond, I think, is important. I don't know if I would still be painting if they were not there.

JP : What if a large percentage of the world began to respond?

MG : I think that would worry me too.

JP : Which brings me to the question about abstraction being elitist.

MG : I don't know if elitist is the right word here. If learning to understand and appreciate Indian classical music is elitist, I suppose abstraction is elitist. I want a viewer who has worked towards responding to my painting.

When my friend the artist Sasha Kolin had a show at a university gallery in New York, one of the curators of the show said that her work passed a simple test: Did the viewer confront the painting? Or was the viewer confronted by the painting? It's a subtle difference. Do you stand in front of a painting and take it in? Or does the painting set the terms by which you will make contact? I don't want to sound precious but a painting must suggest self-containment. A painting must be; it must not seduce.

To me, a reaction coming from someone untutored in the usual clichés of response to contemporary art becomes even more important.

Gopal was a young man who would do some household work for me. Upon my return from a trip to Kangra [in Himachal Pradesh], I had pinned up an attempt I had made to sketch the mountains I could see from my window. I was also working on some totally non-representative abstract studies at the same time. One day, Gopal looked at the landscape and said, "When you can do this, why do you do those?" meaning the abstract work. He was sure I could make a lot of money painting mountains.

Some months later, he began, without knowing it, to respond to the abstract work. He would comment on the colours: "*Yeh rang achcha lagta hai*" (This colour looks good.) Or he would say, "*Isko haath mat lagaaiey*" (Don't touch this one). That's when I confronted him. I said, "You thought I should be painting mountains, remember?" He looked at both again and pointing to the abstract work, he said, "*Isme to haqiqat hai*." (There is reality in this one.)

That response from someone who does not frequent galleries, does not read art criticism, someone who only knew my work and nothing about how it was priced or how it was received, was important. It came, I felt, from the feelings directly evoked by the painting.

JP : And yet you have also spent your life in pursuit of that line.

MG : The edge of a form is a line. I don't see my paintings as being defined by the line as opposed to mass or volume. In my life drawings for instance, yes, there was an elimination of a lot of forms to distil a certain line.

My anatomy teacher at the Art Students League would warn us against producing breasts as circles, boom, boom, nipples as concentric circles. A breast is a muscle, it responds to gravity, it changes shape as the body changes shape, he would say. And Theo Stavropolous who also taught drawing at the university would say that when his female students blurred the penis, he would tell them to treat the testicles as spheres, the penis itself as a cylinder and work with those forms.

It was a time of some prudery in America, in New York too. Male models would often wear briefs or swimming trunks. Then one day, a young man turned up and stripped down and he was nude. I remember Stella, a student who had graduated but who was now monitor of the life drawing class, muttering her disapproval. "Put on your underwear," she told the young man. "Don't have any," he replied and we settled down to drawing him. It was a relief then to be able to draw the torso as an unbroken line, instead of having it cut off by the line of the briefs.

JP : You have done some of the most magnificent life drawings I have seen. They are intimate and impersonal at the same time. They serve as reminders of our common humanity and they also regard the body in terms of pure form. I feel like Gopal here but I am still going to ask: and yet you banished the figure from your work?

MG : To begin with there were abstract representations of the figure, the *Geet Govinda* drawings, for instance. (I had read the George Keyt translation.) Some years ago, when I studied with Shiavax Chavda, one of the exciting things we did was to go for a *Bharata Natyam* performance together. This was my introduction to the form.

As it happens, the great Shanta Rao was performing. We sat in the dark and sketched her as she danced. Her *Bharata Natyam* revealed the pure geometry behind the movements. When she got into *Mohiniattam*, which is more languorous and more seductive, I was not half as excited.

This led me to recognizing the geometry behind the *Chola Nataraja* figure, for instance. It is the compliance with the rules laid down for the creation of such figures that gives them their potency. That a *Chola* bronze represents *Shiva* to the *bhakta* may give it meaning in the context of devotion; but the underlying rigor of its geometry gives it meaningfulness.

JP : I love the story that a collector of yours tells of her throwing open a curtain to reveal a garden in Pune, a garden in full bloom. And Mehlli Gobhai turning from it with the savage dismissal: "Too much colour, too much colour".

How does the painter of abstracts deal with the visual noise, the bright light, the saturation experience of India?

MG : The 'Marking Black' show where I showed with Richard Serra and Sean Scully among others also had a bunch of artists from Israel. They too came from a place saturated with colour and brightness. Yet they too chose to reject colour.

I remember discussing this with these painters who had also chosen to work in black and white. Is it like walking through a sun-drenched field and then resting in the deep shade of a mango tree? Is it like deciding that one will look at black, as in the tantric tradition, as the reservoir of the energies in the universe? Or is it black like a period of silence in music?

JP : So by contrast, the work you're doing now is a riot of colour.

MG : Again, I hope it is colour only when it is necessary.

JP : I remember a time when you were using aluminum powder mixed with acrylic. You could not have known what this would do, how it would work. And yet you did it. In that sense, to experiment means to yield control, to chance failure, to put in a colour that may not be necessary. Could you explain the role of mistakes in your work?

MG : Hugely important. Sasha Kolin would say that if you had worked on a canvas and you found it didn't work, you should simply move away from it and paint another canvas. You shouldn't paint over it.

As an art student in America, I couldn't afford to take that advice and walk away to a new canvas. I had to paint over, and I began to see where pentimenti–the traces of earlier work, of mistakes made, erasures–might add to a panting.

> The erasures and corrections were part of the history of the painting. They were keys to the process. It is important for me that the process shows; they are the signs of the struggle that we were talking about.

JP : I'd like to take you through your process. I know there is an awful lot of gloomy sitting around and looking at the canvas. I know you wipe out, work over, erase, alter, dab, scratch, scrape, incise, work around, work over. I know it all takes a lot of time, much effort, and is the product as much of the mind as it is of the hand and the eye. But can we begin with that moment when the work is about to begin.

MG : It is always a painful, anxiety-ridden moment. The first thing to do is to decide between the potential of a smooth canvas as opposed to the texture of handmade paper which has a life of its own. It takes way from the painting being wholly mine; it's as if some of the work has been done already. Whereas a new canvas is an empty slate. It is I who must create texture here. Then comes for me a time of acute tension: the first line, the first stroke. I am committing myself. I am committing myself to a process that may take months. It may go wrong and I may have to start again and work at erasing what went wrong.
And yes, leaving some of it there.

JP : What function do your notebooks serve?

MG : They're a record of the beginnings and the thinking behind my work. And I'm extremely reluctant to dismember them. When people have wanted to exhibit my notebooks, I have usually refused. I have no problems with friends or collectors leafing through them; it gives them some clues to my process. But I need to have my notebooks on hand because I might find something in them that is relevant now to a painting that I'm working on, even if it is a sketch I did years ago, a thought I wrote down somewhere.

JP : So these are an amalgam of notes and words.

MG : There are words, yes. Some of them are my own. Some are the words of others. They represent a personal archive, I suppose.

JP : An archive might be seen as time condensed and made material. What is the role of time in your work?

MG : I hope that a painting of mine conveys a sense of space and time. I certainly don't want the painting to convey the sense of a quickly-resolved image. I'd like a painting to show the stages of its evolution.

At another level, there is personal time, my time. I remember Raghubir Singh, the photographer, a driven, dedicated artist in his own right. He would stay with us when he was in Bombay and his rolls of film would take up precious space in our refrigerator until he came back and claimed them. Once, on his way out, he stopped at my studio and looked at a work I was doing. "Aah!" he said approvingly, "I don't think you could have done this if you had stayed on in New York."

Then he added, "But I don't think you could have painted like this if you didn't have New York behind you." I liked that.

JP : Your work has moved into the third dimension now with what you describe as the constructed canvases but it always seems to have wanted to break out of the flat pictorial plane.

MG : I think it was in 1994, at the Pundole Art Gallery, that I showed three-dimensional work for the first time in India. 'Hinged by Light', curated by Ranjit Hoskote, brought together works by Prabhakar Kolte, Yogesh Rawal and me.

All three of us worked on pieces that were three dimensional in some way or the other. It was one of the few instances in which a curator worked intensely and consistently with the artists involved. For over a year, we met, talked and shared our work.

Hoskote would say that my work seemed to be heading in that direction. There was an urge to experiment with painting as sculpture.

Ranjit Hoskote wrote about this in 2002:

In the studio, before being set in frames, they possess a free-hanging, sculptural quality. And while Gobhai's concern with the worked-over surface keeps him wedded to the two-dimensional space of the painting, his preoccupation with structure ought to urge him in the direction of the four-dimensional realm of the sculpture-installation, and the re-positioning of his classicism in a new context.

In this sense, I would speculate that these new works are transitional or indexical forms. Pointing beyond the space of painting as they do, I would suggest that they signify the threshold of a new project, a throwing forward of energy into engagement with untested situations. Mehlli Gobhai has not yet permitted himself to articulate these possibilities, but his recent works indicate that he has begun, to adapt a vivid Gutai phrase, "to hear the scream of the material".

JP : One of your friends recently wrote to you that he found your work elegiac.

MG : I like the word elegiac. It speaks to me of emotion filtered through craft. I wish there were fewer high screams of melodrama and more of the power of chanting in modern painting.

In the chant, sorrow is controlled, contained and attains power because it is turned into something more than itself.

The chant repeats itself and possibly serves some therapeutic function; the chant goes back to the Vedas, to prehistory; the chant intensifies emotion and evokes it in the hearer; the chant contains and connects.

Conversation with

Ganesh Haloi

Kolkata 2005

"Every painting has a rhythm. Whether its abstract work or realistic or figurative work, rhythm is a must"

Ganesh Haloi: I have gradually reached this stage, with time. It is a natural process, governed by time. With time, everything gets transformed. Things change. You cannot hold onto anything, uncertainty makes life interesting, worth living. Art critics, historians, theoreticians will observe these changes and define some logic but being a painter yourself you do not know how the changes came about. Change is a natural phenomena, it holds true. So I don't really know how I came to this stage of painting what I am today.

Jesal Thacker: I am interested in finding out what drives you to paint.

GH : A question I get asked very commonly is 'What is painting?' Sometimes, it is posed as 'What is Art?' When I have to face these questions, I tell them that these questions came much later, much after the process of painting had begun. I was simply painting, unconsciously reaching something. So the answer to these questions is different from time to time as it is different from artist to artist. The things that have caused the changes in my work have been different at different stages. The things that have affected my process, that have inspired me to paint have been different from time to time.

JT : But there are external influences on the making of a painting.

GH : Yes that happens. Even by seeing art we learn. Seeing a lot of things you feel inspired, you want to paint. But that does not mean you are copying.

JT : I remember I had listened to a cassette of yours from the time you had a conversation with Prabhakar Kolte in which you told a story by Rabindranath Tagore about the nature of truth.

GH : Yes that is one of my favourite stories. That happens quite often you know, when you read stories by people that you relate to, your curiosity, your *jigyasa* is provoked. I like it when I come across something someone else has written that I have always wanted to say. It becomes like a *mantra*. Such instances result in two possibilities: *Mat* and *Mantra.*

Do you know what the difference between the two is? *Mat* refers to individual opinions. They vary; they differ from person to person. As Rama krishna used to say "...there will be as many paths as there are opinions..." But there has to be a common direction. *Mantra* takes you that way. It is an amalgamation of influences that result in a sort of universal rule.

Take the Mughal rule for example. We imbibed certain aspects of it as a part of Indian art. When foreign influence comes into the picture there is a difference in opinions. This difference results in a debate and that which is effective, survives. Thus if you look at art, no one human being is responsible. It has been a collective effort. Whether it is art, literature, science, it is always the entire community that contributes. And when it is a collective contribution the progress becomes apparent. It is that *mantra* that is born of assimilating these influences and gives rise to new thoughts, new art forms.

What is Mughal painting for example? It is the result of elements of Indian art and Persian art coming together. Even when the British came, their opinions came with them. Some people imitated, some rebelled. That rebellion caused a debate and gave rise to a new form of Indian art. It is all a game of *Mat* and *Mantra.*

The *Mantra* remains constant. It is that which inspires. Our mind again operates on two factors: intellect and emotion. When emotion exceeds intellect, we end up getting carried away.

It is the intellect that keeps a check on the mind. But both these factors have to be balanced. Any one of these exceeding the other is unfavorable. We think with our intellect and we work and feel with our emotions. What if emotions were missing? Life would become very stark.

JT : You also used the example of the spoon...

GH : Yes, look at the spoon. How was it designed? Its utility was placed first. How it was to be used determined its design. So the design was thought about before it was executed. But it was also designed so that it looked beautiful. But it's different when it comes to art. When man created objects of utility, he made sure he was not at their mercy. He was not at the mercy of their functionality.

We simply look at the design; we do not look at the utility of objects. Take the example of the border of the *sari*. The border is beautiful but that isn't its function.

The border makes sure that the *sari* remains stiff at the edges so that it can be worn easily. The border gives the *sari* a graceful fall. It makes sure that the *sari* doesn't tear when one walks while wearing it. So the border was born because of its function but its width was increased for beauty. The functional side remained inside; the designed band was kept on the outside.
So we need to remain free of the functionality of the object. We have to keep our aesthetic sense at work. But the balance is a precarious one. We have to be able to maintain it.

No painting is complete without a touch of life. There is a difference between a nicely decorated set of spoons in a shop and those that we use at home. The ones in the shop are deprived of human company, of emotion; whereas our moods vary at home.

We might pick up the spoon when sad, some other times while happy. Each time the touch varies. It gives life to the spoon.

A relation of exchanging emotions is established when the spoon comes in contact with human company. If we follow this chain of the process of the formation of the relationship, you will see it give rise to a drawing. For example, follow your journey to Calcutta. You caught a plane in Bombay and landed here, and then you went to some other place, finished up with your work there, then came to my house and are recording this conversation.

Life is full of these paths and lines. If you keep tracing your movements back in time, numerous such paths will be formed.

In fact, I will go further and say that life itself is a line. Only this line should be rhythmic. If the line of your life is rhythmic, you will definitely enjoy it, otherwise you won't. There is no fun without rhythm.

Every painting has a rhythm. Whether its abstract work or realistic or figurative work, rhythm is a must, isn't it? I was once approached to speak at a course on Indian art. I have always questioned this concept.

Why Indian art? Why not simply art? Where will you draw the line, how do you define such a thing? How do you decide where Indian art begins and where it ends? Yes, but I am still aware of the fact that no matter how much I communicate in English, there is something intrinsically Indian inside me. I don't know where I have absorbed it from, tradition, history, culture but it is there all the same. It is what we absorb from living here. It is not something that shows or that can be shown. It is there. I like belonging here. I like Indian philosophy, it is very rich. I would never want to leave the country.

There is a story of a student who once asked his teacher about philosophy saying 'Where is God? We can't see Him. We can't feel Him. How do we know He is there?' The teacher replied, 'Look at Nature. It is made up of *vikriti* - transformation. Everything is interchangeable. Trees, leaves, the soil, the clouds...everything. Thus, even if you paint a leaf, there is God in it." Don't we believe there is *brahma* in everything?

I consider myself fortunate that I arrived in the world with the gift of art. I don't have to work at a job to earn my living. My time is my own. There are no external pressures. The progress of my work depends entirely on my inner realization process.

I simply have to follow my path, which I believe in and it will take me to that ultimate goal where there is God and where I hope to surrender to him. It is okay to talk but only talking will get you no where! It's a bit like realism. Realism doesn't fuel any growth. How has the earth become so beautiful? Can we be realistic about things like this? The earth was not made beautiful by realism but by imagination!

Tell me, what is the ultimate goal in life? You want to be happy, right? Using your imagination makes you happy. When you're working on a painting, and it turns out exactly as it planned, it isn't that satisfying. When the painting turns out to be something you least expected that's when you're filled with that ultimate exhilaration!

Because it is unexpected...it is new. Because you realize that the elements that you use in your painting have begun to respond to you in harmony. I find harmony responding to me so many times. Harmony between form, line, colour, tension...if there is harmony, the painting works.

But many times the environment affects us. Take, for example, a building like a fortress. Let us say it is one that has thick walls, huge Gothic pillars, heavy architecture. Automatically there is a pressure that the building exerts on us. There are certain vibrations that you sense there. And there is a certain way in which I respond to these vibrations.

Now if I walk into a contemporary building, I am going to react differently to the vibrations I get there. Each of these exists through their vibrations. The vibrations prove their existence. And I can sense these vibrations only when I am free of preconceived ideas.

JT : What inspires you to paint?

GH : If f I don't paint, everything will become static. The source of inspiration as well as the process of pursuing it differs from person to person. Tell me, how many gods are there? One, right? But look at the number of ways of praying to him. There are so many different kinds of prayers! And yet there is one very important thing you must maintain: your presence should not be apparent. Your identity does not matter.

The artist shouldn't get carried away with trying to establish his style. This is true for anyone who does creative work. Gradually, before you realize it, in an effort to maintain your style you end up getting mechanical.

Everything is up to me. I am my own master. No one dictates what I have to do. No one has put a gun to my back and asked me to follow a particular path. Every creative person should have his/her own independent creative process. Life should be flowing; all the uncertainty along the way is the fun of it. You come across new observations as you go along. Similarly, painting is a process of realization.

A song sung from the beginning to the end occupies time in space. A story told from the beginning to its end occupies time in space. Now look at the function of the dot and the line. A dot holds you still whereas the line gives you a direction.

What does a painting do? It makes you still in time and as you continue to observe it, it takes you forward and backward: within. Where else can you witness such magic? The painting takes you into your *bhavajagat*, your world of emotions. You have to finish listening to the entire story or song but with a painting, the reaction happens simultaneously with the observing process.

JT : Yesterday you were saying that everything comes from certainty to uncertainty.

GH: The game between uncertainty and certainty gives life its colour. But the journey has to be focused. Take this object for example. That can be our reference point. There is a certain distance between the object and me. Thus there is also a tension. To reach that object, I have to travel through this tension. The various factors of a painting can be balanced with a sense of this tension. Things move forward because of it. There is a tension among us as well, right? Even if we do not talk, if we keep silent, even then there is a dialogue.

The distance in terms of time and space separate the object from me. But there are subtler ways of reaching it other that physically. If I set my mind to it, all these barriers get destroyed!! The object then reveals itself to me.

You can follow the principle of this tension with the example of a hunter who spots a deer. He intensifies the tension between them when he points it out and takes aim. If he uses the right force he strikes it, if he mistakes the distance that is the tension the deer gets away!

The distribution of the factors that constitute a painting creates a design. There is a design in every painting. The design is a must. The design holds the life, *chetana*

I have to be conscious about what touches my viewers. I have to be aware of what they like about my work. Because I would like to paint something that reaches my viewers. I like it when my thoughts match with another person's. I want to communicate.

GH : With certainty, you get stuck at one place, because everything becomes too definite, certain.
And if uncertainty doesn't come again, you remain static.

The journey, from certainty to uncertainty is what makes life wonderful. Then again certainty will replace that uncertainty because you find some answers. If this doesn't go on continuously, where is the momentum in life?

JT : That can be seen in your paintings. You return to explore things again and again.

GH : One thing can be looked at from ten different angles. If you look out of my window upstairs during the day, you can see trees, birds. You can see a landscape.

I have made so many paintings from the same window but no two paintings are alike. No one has set any rules for you. No one has assigned you with anything definite to paint. Nature is original. Don't imitate it. All the great painters have painted nature and avoided imitating it.

Look at Da Vinci, Michelangelo. Michelangelo did not imitate nature. He painted his interpretation of it; he gave it the emotion that his subject created in him. His style may be realistic but you have to see the spirit of the work. His paintings were not like photographs.When you look at Rembrandt's work, aren't you surprised? Even when I see miniature paintings, I am awestruck.

After the Ajanta paintings were done, even after the classical period the transformation that miniature painting through is amazing. All those schools, *Kishingadh, Malwa, Kangra*... it was all so interesting that in my third year I went and bought a book on miniature paintings.

I chose not to make distinctions like Western paintings and Indian paintings. Painting is painting. A lot of people like to differentiate art like that. They make categories for all kinds of works that have been done. But you cannot call something Western art and something else Indian art.

It is not the effort of one particular man or one particular group. It is the collective effort of society. Everything has happened as a whole.

JT : You spoke about necessary elements in painting. That painting has its own language. So far we have been talking about the philosophy of art. Now let's talk about your painting.A painter chooses one or two particular elements he wants to explore in his painting.

For example, Ram Kumar says that he is exploring colour in his paintings. He finds the mystery of colour intriguing. This exploration of his is clear in the compositions on his canvas. Is there such an element for you, something you are going deeper into?

GH : Yes, of course colour is important to me. But I begin with thinking about the space. The square, the rectangle that I am about to fill. I look at that space first. Often, while observing it I find that the space itself guides me. Whatever I make is according to the space. This space is what possesses vital force.

For example, let's say there is a piece of land that you want to cultivate. How will you cultivate it? You will have to plan the manner as well as the pattern of cultivation. You will have to say that this is where I will plant a tree. This is where I will build a house. The garden will come here. Which, to put it simply, means that you will divide the space. That comes first for me. After that I think about what I want to make.

My paintings are mostly concerned with nature. But nobody will look at my painting and say that this is a subjective, figurative composition. They will say that it is a painting with some resemblance to a landscape. But this resemblance is not 'as it is'. Something is definitely common but it is not just the physical appearance.

I try to make an effort to paint something that I got from nature but is not like nature. I try to paint a land that is my own.

JT: Your land?

GH: My land. With my rules. It has no resemblance to nature. It is the struggle to create this land that makes the process of painting interesting. The space tension with the object has to be maintained.

Rhythm is another important factor in the painting. Look at Kolte's paintings. They have rhythm. There can be no painting without rhythm. There is no life without rhythm. Now where did this rhythm come from?

Think of man in his primitive stage. Life was a struggle. Human beings were scared of the forests. Before they started to build houses, they would take shelter in caves. They were always filled with a kind of fear.

They had to constantly fight with nature. But they did hunt for food. That was an exciting event. So they painted it. Parts of it were good, parts of it were not, but the question is how did they achieve it and what did they get out of it.

There is a silent movement that we subconsciously respond to. That is how man could simply look at the kind of day it was and predict accurately whether it was going to rain or not. The sky, the trees, everything was understood by instinct. Instinct is what is almost destroyed now. We could foretell the events of the next day based on these instincts. It was this instinct that we got from nature. How much has nature taught us?

It has given us the silent sound from which rhythm is born. We cannot hear it because it is silent, but it exists

The rhythm is what makes things work, gives things pattern. When we responded to rhythm with our bodies, we learned to dance. Or else how would a primitive man learn to dance.

When we respond to that sound with our voices, with notes, music was created. And when we experienced that sense of wonder and wanted to express it ourselves, it came in the form of painting. We have taught ourselves how to paint. Singing, dancing, painting - all forms of creation - has all come to us. This is how it all began. This is what we mean when we say that culture has followed a course and brought us where we are today. Even today, when we paint something that lacks this rhythm, we feel dissatisfied. We finish the painting and put it aside. It is painful to even look at it until you enter that rhythm.

I'll try to be more specific about what I mean by rhythm. Let's see: This object is placed here. Nanak is sitting here, I am here and you are there. There is a table between us. There is a glass, a flowerpot with a flower on the table. If I decide to place it all in white space, where will I place it all. This is space division. The tension that exists in space, between the object and the space, between objects, which gives it an identity. It is not dead. There is a connection. I am with it.

So, when I paint, what will I do with this connection? That is when the problem arises. The problem only gets solved when a balance is achieved, when there is a rhythmic harmony. It is in this rhythmic harmony that we want to speak; we want to express. Otherwise, there is no expression. Things get made but there is no expression. If I place three straight lines like this, the letter H is created. So according to me, at the same time a design as well as a composition has been created. This miracle called nature is unlimited. I believe in it. We have to preserve our sense of wonder.

I asked myself how do I look at everything in the world? What have I learned? Who taught me things as a child? How does a child learn how to walk? Nobody has to teach him, he learns so many things on his own.

In fact there are a whole lot of things that we learn on our own. Some things we learn through reading; some we learn from nature.

What if we decide to forget all the things we have learned later and go right back to the basics? We are left with the basic forms and structures in nature. We cannot go beyond them. What are these basic structures?

For example something stands. It is vertical in nature, now even if the shape leans towards being horizontal in nature its direction is still vertical, right?

So this vertical line becomes a basic form. If this slanting diagonal gets joined to it, it looks like the branch of a tree. We have seen this; nobody has to teach us this. We see it all around us. It exists in nature. There, if this diagonal crosses this other diagonal it clearly begins to look like a tree; branches cross each other like this. So the diagonal line exists in nature. There is a straight line; there is a horizontal line...

JT : The horizon.

GH : See, when a man stands erect it is a vertical, when he dies it is a horizontal. I thought a lot about this. About what the exact thought process is but I realized that we don't go beyond this.

Look at this shape of a pyramid—it's like a mountain. Anything with height in nature looks like this. Even if you pour things, like rice or pulses—anything at all, it will acquire this pyramid shape because of gravity. After that there is 'round'. A bubble is round, a drop of water lands and forms a circle.

There is another basic form in nature and that is the rhythmic line. A wave on the surface of water is a rhythmic line. When the wind blows through trees a rhythmic line is created. When the sand dunes move in the desert, a rhythmic line is created.

When you show this kind of line to children, they immediately call it water. Children use a lot of basic forms while drawing. When they draw faces, they draw a frontal view. They hardly ever draw a profile. You draw two dots with another dot below them at the center—a face is formed. Two horizontal lines emerging from the round of the face make the hands. Then a vertical line drawn straight below makes the body. Younger kids just draw that much.

Then they begin to realize that there is waist in the human body, there are legs and they begin to divide their line into these parts.

Gradually, the picture grows. They look at basic forms as pieces. They think of assembling them to create whatever they want to. Then they begin to grow up and reach the age of 8 or 9 years. This is a very bad age. This is the age when they begin to feel disappointed because the cow they draw doesn't look like a cow, a man they draw doesn't look like a man. They come closer to reality as they grow up.

So they want to be able to paint everything as it is. They want it all to look 'natural'. They lose their sense of basic form.

There is another important aspect that we have to consider here. The movement of our neck—it moves only in a certain way, along a particular axis. So since we are used to looking around only in a certain manner, looking at a tall skyscraper becomes difficult. We don't see these squares and rectangles in nature but we do see them in a book which is manmade. When pre historic man lived in caves, he began to draw. They apparently drew hunting scenes. But they never drew a frame around them! They only thought of making frames after they began to make houses.

Have you seen any primitive paintings with frames? There was a seminar held once on primitive art. Even there the historian pointed out that the concept of the frame came only after man got civilized. He made tables, he made books...

JT : Even the Indus Valley seals are square shaped.

GH: Yes, houses had been made by then. That was when the concept of planning had already come into society. By then man had begun to use the square as though it was the basic form. But it is not a basic form. We are using to create and are forcing ourselves into employing something that is not fundamental in nature. It is forced, not natural.

JT: What is the difference between 'forced' and 'natural'?

GH : Forced implies the situation in which people tell themselves that they just have to do something new for the sake of it. If he has made the eye like that, I will make it like this, different from him to be better than him. But he doesn't think beyond that. He doesn't think about any radical changes. So he paints the eye differently but in its own place. So on one hand he tries to be different and on the other he follows reality.

Look at the kind of figures Jogen Chowdhury paints today. He paints them for a reason. But there are artists who follow him just for the sake of following a trend. They think that is creative.

You know Vanita? She had once said something that made a lot of sense to me. She said that there once was a rose bush and a jasmine plant. They spring from the same soil. And yet are so different from each other because they follow different processes.

It is their processes that come out as their form. This is nature. It has to be like this, natural. It has to happen on its own. The shapes have to form on their own, the form has to possess an intrinsic growth. Okay, now look at this square. I draw this vertical line inside it with these two diagonals on top and this horizontal line below. Then I draw this circle in the top right corner and this rhythmic, wavy line at the bottom. This pyramid here...It is just about space division.

Now if I ask someone what this is, they will say it is clearly a landscape. This is a tree, this is water, this is a mountain, this is the sun...any ordinary person would respond this way. And it is right too. Because where has it all come from? From nature itself.

It was in nature and it has come from nature. And there have been certain concepts in our mind that make us place these basic elements in a certain way.
We will never make this vertical line float like this in the air; we will show it touching the ground. Because we have always been aware of gravitation. We will show it rooted, on a surface. That will form the base. If it is shown floating, it seems like magic to the ordinary person. Like someone dropped it from top and it never fell, just kept hanging. People get surprised. Instead if I draw it like this, touching the base it looks nice, it feels nice. Why do you think that happens?

JT : Because we are used to seeing it this way.

GH : Because we see it around us on the earth. Because it is found in nature. It matches with reality as we know it and therefore we accept it. And it is this reality that we are unable to abandon. Okay, now look at this. This is the base.

Now instead of drawing a line going upwards just like that, I give it a break. Suppose I give it a break here and here and then continue it, does it make a difference? It does, doesn't it? Now which of these designs would you like?

Ask any one who does ordinary work. They will like this one because it is closest to reality. It is in harmony with nature. This one with the form in the centre doesn't appeal to us because we are not used to seeing any ordinary object placed in the centre in nature.

Whom do we place in the centre? Gods and goddesses. Okay now if I put this line here, it looks better doesn't it? If I leave this area empty, it doesn't look nice. If I pull this further below it looks even better. Why? Because a connection is being established with the earth.

We always associate the base line with the ground, the earth. It looks rooted and therefore we accept it. When you do interior designing isn't this one of the things you have to keep in mind? This kind of basic space division exists in all our paintings. It has been brought about automatically in some cases, out of pure instinct.

When there is no rhythm among the forms we use, it makes the viewer uncomfortable. That is why using squares is risky. They don't work. They end up looking static. A circle is okay. But again, if you join a circle to a square underneath, that will look acceptable too. Because we associate it immediately with a vehicle's wheel and therefore mobility.

Everything ultimately comes from nature. What isn't there in nature? There's small, big, tiny, giant, thin, fat, protruding, recessing; then there's smooth, there's rough....This texture plays a very important role in painting.

Another extremely important factor is pressure. Whenever there is emotion, there is pressure. I'll give you a simple example. There is an association of pressure with each object that we use.

Look at this pencil. Unless I apply pressure, an impression will not be formed from the lead. Unless I rub it on the paper with pressure, there will be no image.

That stain, which is formed as a result of pressure, is what carries that texture that we were referring to.

Hope is a very important element.
Hope and desire. Unless there is strong desire, that struggle to achieve something will not come. Then there will be a force, a momentum in your life. But it has to be the right kind of desire, positive desire.

As I have mentioned earlier, the desire to paint is principally governed by two factors: emotion and intellect. Only when emotion and intellect reach equilibrium, does a painting get completed. The emotion controls the intensity of feeling in the painting while intellect gives it the structure.

When I make a design, yes it does have reason in it but unless it experiences a touch of life it cannot truly become a painting. That touch of life...touch of feeling is what makes the painting universal. It should reach everyone. How is it going to reach everyone when every individual is different from one another?

We need to understand that this difference lies in the intellects. Intellectually, each person is different but on an emotional level we are all similar. Because that is reaching on the inside and if this wasn't the case, we wouldn't find only a few paintings worth looking at. We feel drawn only to those paintings in which there is truth...there is honesty.

It need not all be about 'nice' 'good' things... even if it is about the bad things in life it will appeal to us if it is expressed honestly. These days a lot of artists find themselves painting about sex. Yes...it is a subject...but again if the expression is meaningful the painting speaks of it...if it is not then it comes across as mere perversion. That quality of being meaningful is the painting's connection with life.

Everyone is walking at his pace, in his way. Thus the work we produce differs in terms of forms, subjects, isms, schools. But that constant struggle to find the meaning, that honesty, should become a way of life.

Conversation with

Prabhakar Kolte

Mumbai 2005

> "I feel the world which is in front of my eyes but I also feel the one that does not exist. I have a great curiosity regarding that world"

Jesal Thacker: I remember you saying that a lot of introverted artists happen to be abstract painters. Do you think that is more than a coincidence?

Prabhakar Kolte: Let me begin by speaking for myself. I have a certain nature. It is who I am. For instance, I do not like traveling but I have to. Often, I find myself traveling so much that people say, 'Hey! You are always away.' But I like to work within the ambit of four walls. This in itself is neither right nor wrong.

But for the purposes of argument, let us assume a division of the world into an external and an internal. The external world is concrete, tangible. It is the world with which you must communicate.

You learn many things from it and you feel that it is life; you develop a trust in its empirical nature. Whatever talent you have to show has to be done in this life.

So, your activity is extroverted. Your activity is related to an external world. It may have a quality of introspection but its base is in reality. And yet I would say that my paintings are not related to the external world. Perhaps they have progressed from the external towards internal but it is not related to the external. Do you understand the statement, art for art sake? I support this opinion. But this does not mean that I am not at all related to the external world. For practical reasons, I am. This modern materialistic world has some function in my life; but my life is not based on it.

My creativity, my thoughts are not related to that world. But I would not say that if another artist were to take cognizance of that world, he would be wrong. It is only another approach, another point of view.

I feel the world which is in front of my eyes but I also feel the one that does not exist. I have a great curiosity regarding that world. From where do these shapes evolve, this concrete human form, animals, trees?

Science tells us all these shapes that we see have evolved from amoeba. The amoeba had no shape;

so what came before the amoeba? This question haunts me. I try to find this world in my paintings. Some people like to represent the world that they see; they may even seek to interpret it. Some are inspired by it and might like to express it.

I want to say that I see all this, observe it. I collect everything but my thoughts, my feelings, what I want to do, is not related to this. If I have to put it in the language of the materialistic world, then a useful analogy would be that of colour and form, because they are external. They are not produced internally.
Colour has to be squeezed out of the tube. It has materialistic application.

I feel everything is basically abstract. Even figurative drawing to begin with is abstract because there are only lines and colours. Steadily, it gets a shape, steadily it gets an identity Basically all this is abstract. The world lies in an atom; there is nothing concrete as such.

JT : What is abstract to you?

PK : Perhaps I could begin by talking about impressionism. What was the problem they were confronting? The camera had been invented. It had usurped art's function of representation. They though, 'If we work in the same way, people might laugh.

They might say: the camera can do in two minutes what you take two months over.'

An artist is basically a thinker.

But at that time his thoughts are not on the surface Perhaps they wondered: 'Should we continue doing whatever we did?

Perhaps they were responding to the particular quality of light in Europe. There, light is momentary; one moment you have light and the next moment it is dark, it rains, you feel cold. To paint you need light. And there, the light flickers, on and off. Here in Mumbai we take light for granted, it's sunny and it goes on being sunny. So their aim was to paint this light, the light that came and went and eluded them. Their drawings have mistakes but that may have because they weren't really bothered about the drawing as they pursued light. Perhaps a critic thought 'Oh! This is an impression of a landscape' and he called it impressionism.

Remember, none of the original Impressionists as we know them thought they were constructing impressionism. Their aim was to paint light and the effects of light. That was the concept .Impressionism was not the concept. In a painting itself there are various concepts.

Some people like to paint with watercolours. That is a kind of choice, a choice based on concepts. I like watercolours. I used them till recently because I thought that it was a question of my temperament. I was doing oil paintings till 1986, but I had to stop. That made me lose my creativity. Then painting became an exercise on the canvas. It would be an action, not a painting. I found that I like working fast. It suits my temperament. I like to finish a work in one mood, whether it takes three hours or three days. And there again watercolours suited me.

But this again is derived from my attitude to life, it is derived from my approach to art, from history, from aesthetics and so many other factors. I thought, 'Yes, somewhere all these things together make me want to say something'.

And of course there were influences of people like Gaitonde, Raza, Husain, Paul Klee, Palsikar, etc... you know they matter a lot. All of them have given worth to my concept of abstraction. We call it abstraction but that is just convenient; everyone thinks they know what is abstract.

My concept is different. For me it is just a painting. I don't want to name it. I don't want to put it into some compartment. I don't think calling it 'abstraction' is correct. It is just a painting, that which I can see, that which everyone can see and enjoy, it is so simple. But we call it 'abstraction' because everyone is familiar with the term 'abstraction'.

JT : But these conveniences have become part of usage in the world of art, haven't they?
For example, if I want to study impressionism, irrespective of whether I relate to the term or not, I know whether a painting can be called impressionistic or not, I know whether a painter can be called an impressionist or not. So today if I want to study these people who are painting nonfigurative works with a similar line of thought, they are grouped together under the term 'abstraction.' What would you say about your own work?

PK : Before we come to my work, I would tell you to look at Kandinsky's work, see Paul Klee and then see my work or anybody else's work. These people are the founders of abstraction. So you will find a landscape in Kandinsky's paintings. And he has simplified that landscape. While simplifying, he concentrated on the basic elements....line, form, colour.

It means he has not drawn a mountain, but a triangle. Then even that triangle left and just triangular lines remained. Initially, you can see trees, maybe a horse, but not later. Colours came in and went on becoming so simplified that it resulted in form. That is abstraction. It has its roots in the external world: a landscape.

Paul Klee said that simplifying the world is not abstraction. What is the language of the artist? Line, form, color and texture. These are his alphabet. I have to present my experience based on these letters, says Paul Klee.

I think I understood what Paul Klee meant when he said that painting has its own language so it should not imitate the nature.

Paul Klee said we should create like nature. What does it mean to create like nature? And I thought 'Yes, I should follow nature'. Until then, I only imitated. But he said that we should follow nature, that we are nature, a part of nature living in nature. So we should follow nature and one day we will create as she does.

Now I have realized the difference between 'following' and 'imitating'. If I am following nature and I am nature, then to follow nature is to follow myself.

So nature is not outside. It is as much outside as it is inside; then I realized I have suddenly transformed the whole world, whatever is seen. This tree, which you can see, is not nature; it's the footprint left by the nature. I was once five years old and now I am sixty, there is a difference, isn't there?

My body is the same but it goes on changing but still I am in front of you. That is the effects of nature. Nature is about growth and movement. I wanted to understand that movement, that inner movement.

JT : Your paintings always seem in search of something...

PK : Searching for myself rather.

JT : They seem to be attempting to create another parallel world..

PK : Absolutely! The nature of nature.

JT : In your painting, what is your language?

PK : My alphabet is the same as any painter, as Paul Klee
said.

I include in my work my inner voice, my inner search. That is why my painting is never complete. I know it is complete in one sense because after a point I don't feel like working on it.

My painting has no beginning.
It has only a beginning in the
material sense that I do
something on paper, but when
it begins, it goes on as the life
goes on.
Life continues even in sleep.
Am I dead if I sleep? No.
Breathing continues.
Thoughts continue.
Likewise painting goes on.
Painting doesn't stop but I do.
I decide that I don't want to
continue further; that is an
aesthetic decision.

JT : So when do you do that?

PK : Sometimes it is just lethargy, sometimes like turning a page of the same novel. But I feel that earlier my answers were different; then I had different understanding.

Do you understand? Now I know for myself that my painting has no end because it has no beginning. When I did not know how to paint, it was still there in me. When I was not painting, even then I was doing it internally.

JT : It is more of a searching process than finding.

PK : My painting is my search; it is lifelong, a constant search. Whatever happens to the observer happens to me.